Hide-and-Seek Visual Adventures

UNCOVER
TECHNOLOGY

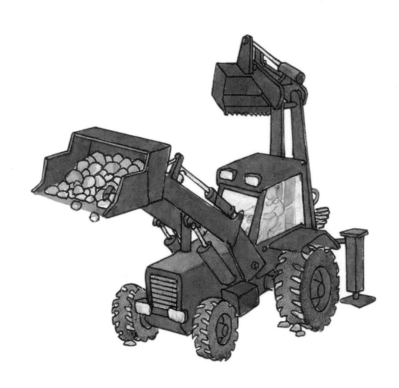

Published in 2010 by Windmill Books, LLC
303 Park Avenue South, Suite 1280
New York, NY 10010-3657

First published in 2009 by Orpheus Books Ltd.,
6 Church Green, Witney, Oxfordshire, OX28 4AW

Created and produced by Nicholas Harris, Sarah Hartley, Erica Williams, and Katie Sexton
Orpheus Books Ltd.

Illustrated by Peter Kent

Text by Olivia Brookes

Library of Congress Cataloging-in-Publication Data

Brookes, Olivia.
Uncover technology / [text by Olivia Brookes] ; illustrated by Peter Kent.
p. cm. -- (Hide-and-seek visual adventures)
Includes bibliographical references and index.
ISBN 978-1-60754-658-0 (library binding : alk. paper)
1. Technology--Juvenile literature. I. Peter Kent. II. Title.

T48.B856 2010
600--dc22

2009032842

Printed and bound in China

CPSIA compliance information: Batch # OR9002019: For further information contact Windmill Books, New York, New York at 1-866-478-0556.

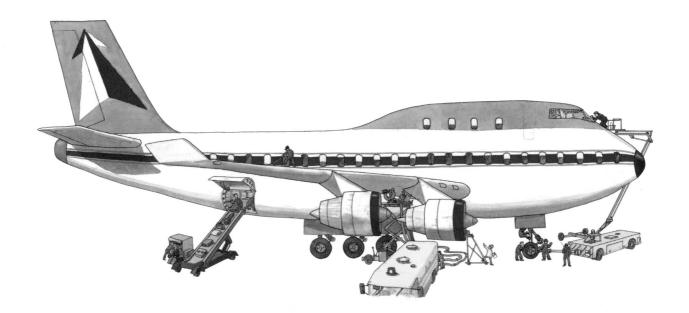

Hide-and-Seek Visual Adventures

UNCOVER TECHNOLOGY

Illustrated by Peter Kent

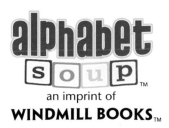

alphabet
soup™

an imprint of
WINDMILL BOOKS™

Contents

Introduction

This book takes you on a trip to some interesting places. You visited a city or a farm, or traveled on an airliner, but chances are you have not yet journeyed into space! The illustrator has taken off the

walls of some of the buildings and the sides off some of the machines pictured in this book. This means you have the special treat of being able to look inside them. Now you can watch the workers on a construction site or the farmer milking cows. You can also take a close look at an airliner's engines, the flight deck of a Space Shuttle, or the engine room of a large ferry. Look in the index to find other things you'd like to see.

Look out for this pesky frog! He is hidden in every scene...

Airliner

An airliner can carry hundreds of passengers to different parts of the world. It has very powerful jet engines attached to each wing. They blast out hot air, driving the plane forward.

Rudder

Tailfin

Terminal building

Control tower

Luggage

Cargo hold

Landing gear

The passengers' luggage is stowed in the airliner's cargo hold before take-off. The ground crew use this special moving ramp. It carries bags and suitcases up to the hold by a conveyor belt.

Many different vehicles are used to keep things running smoothly at an airport. These mechanical road sweepers keep the runway clear, so the aircraft can take off and land smoothly.

The wheels on an aircraft are called its landing gear. A jumbo jet has 18 giant wheels. They are all needed to carry its enormous weight.

The pilot and co-pilot sit at the controls on the flight deck. The passengers sit in the cabin, where they are looked after by the flight attendants. In this airliner, known as a jumbo jet, the passenger cabins are on two decks.

Airliner taking off

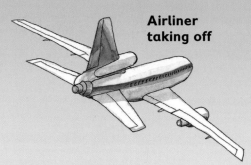

Terminal building

Pilots' bunks

Flight deck

Passenger cabin

Engine

Fuel tanker

Mobile crane

A jumbo jet is powered by turbofans, a kind of jet engine. Hot exhaust gas escapes at high speeds out of the back of the engine. The backward-flowing air peopels the plan forward.

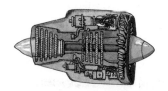

Air traffic controllers work inside a control tower. They direct aircraft to and from the runways. They decide when it is safe to take off or land.

To take off, an airliner races at high speed down the runway. Its wings are shaped so that air moving over the wing moves faster than the air beneath it. This provides a force called lift. The airliner will climb into the air if the lift is greater than its weight.

Space Shuttle

The Space Shuttle is a spacecraft that is designed to travel into space over and over again. It can carry satellites, which are placed in orbit around Earth. It also takes people up to repair those satellites, or to visit the International Space Station, where they carry out experiments.

At lift-off, the orbiter (pictured here) is attached to two booster rockets and a huge fuel tank. After they blast the shuttle into space, these fall back to Earth. At the end of its mission, the Space Shuttle orbiter glides back home to Earth and lands on a runway just like an airliner.

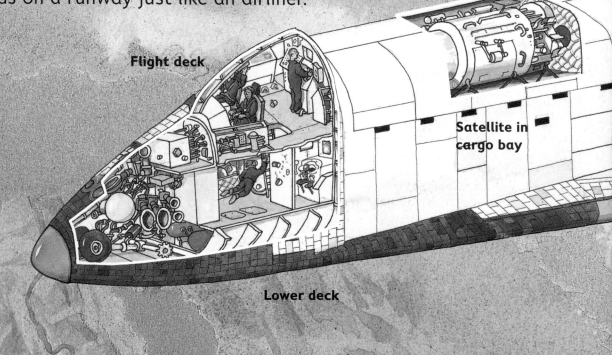

Flight deck

Satellite in cargo bay

Lower deck

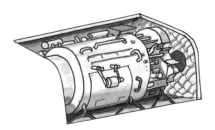

Satellites are released into space to send back information to Earth. They have many uses, including weather forecasting, television signals, and Sat Nav.

In a rocket engine, two different fuels mix together and react in a combustion chamber. The explosive reaction creates hot gases that blast out of a nozzle at great speed. This propels the shuttle up and away!

The flight deck is like the cockpit of an airplane. It contains the controls for the Shuttle. The astronauts use footstraps to keep their feet on the floor.

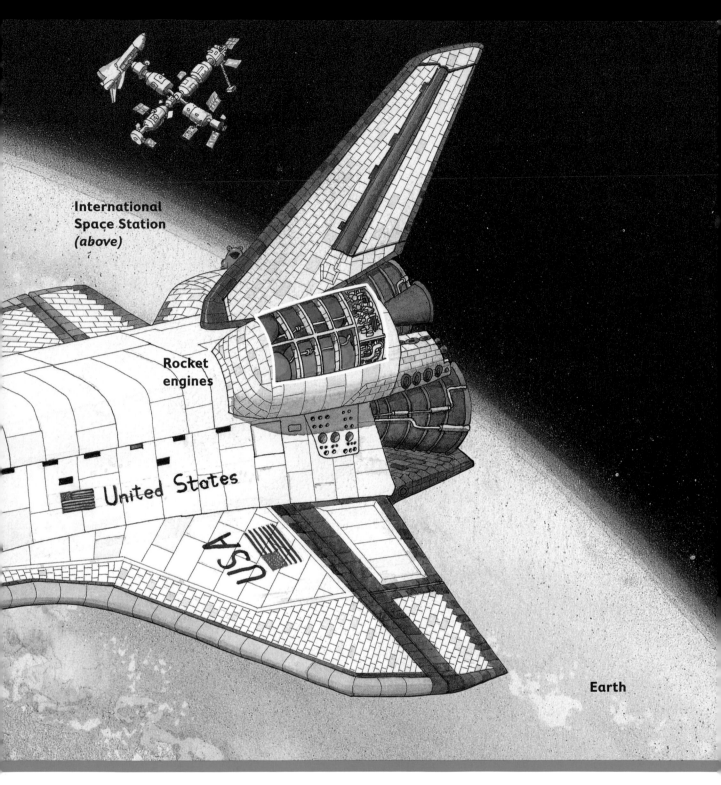

International Space Station (above)

Rocket engines

United States

USA

Earth

The lower deck is where the crew's living quarters are located. Here there are beds and a toilet. While in orbit, the astronauts (and everything else) are completely weightless.

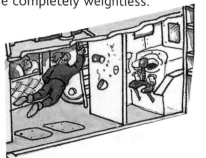

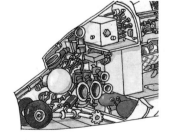

Located in the nose of the Space Shuttle are the forward control thrusters. These allow it to make maneuvers while in space.

Orbiting high above the Earth is the International Space Station. Here, scientists conduct experiments to try to find out how living things survive in space.

Ferry

This ferry carries people and their cars across the sea. The passengers can walk around the top deck and look at the view.

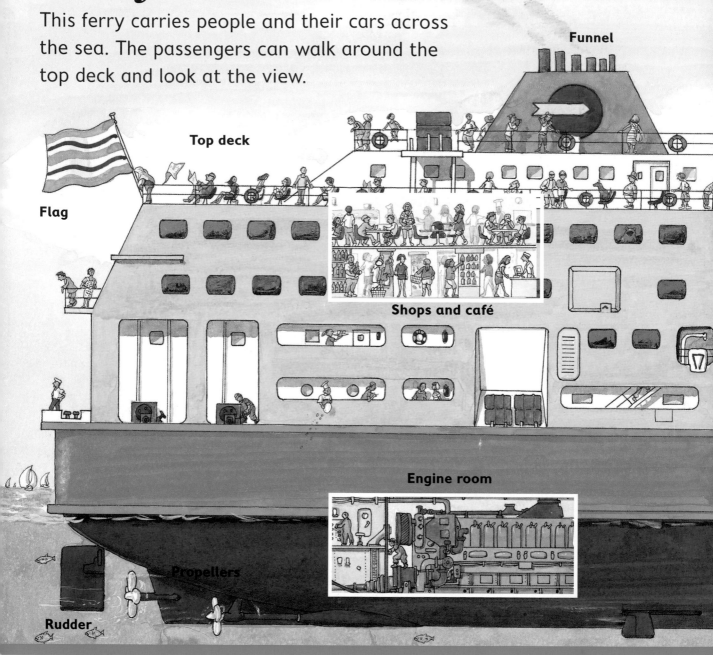

Funnel

Top deck

Flag

Shops and café

Engine room

Propellers

Rudder

Passengers leave their cars on the lower decks. Trucks park on the lowest decks because they are heaviest. When the ferry arrives, the passengers go to their cars and drive down a ramp off the ship.

Lifeboats are carried on a ferry so that passengers can escape to safety if there is an emergency. They are lowered from the top deck to the sea via pulleys. Lifeboats usually carry several days' supply of food and water.

A large ferry is almost like a small town. Besides restaurants, bars, and shops, it might also have a movie theater, a gym, a swimming pool, and an amusement arcade.

Some ferry journeys can take a long time and passengers might need to sleep overnight. There are small cabins complete with beds and a bathroom below deck.

Radar

Bridge

Lifeboat

Vehicle decks

The ferry's engines drive the propellers, which power the ship through the water. To go faster, the engine's throttle is opened up, making the engine work harder and the propeller turn faster.

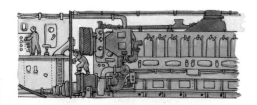

The propellers' blades are large and curved. As they turn, the water around them is sucked in and pushed backward. This drives the ship forward.

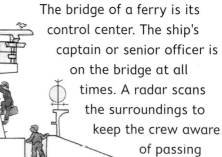

The bridge of a ferry is its control center. The ship's captain or senior officer is on the bridge at all times. A radar scans the surroundings to keep the crew aware of passing ships and their exact position at sea.

City

Cities are busy places. There are many cars, trucks, buses, and taxis driving along the streets. The sidewalks are crowded with people shopping or walking to work. Cities can be very noisy places, too. You can always hear the revving of engines or the beeping of horns.

Market

Bus

Gas station

Bike

People fly all over the world to visit cities. They often need to stay in a hotel for a few nights. Besides rooms, large hotels have many facilities including a restaurant, bar, gym, and swimming pool.

Parking garages are made up of many floors on top of one another. This saves space in busy downtown areas. To park or exit, drive up or down a spiral ramp from one floor to the next.

Offices are found in cities. Roads and trains are crowded every morning and evening as people travel to and from work.

At the market, there are stalls selling all kinds of things: fresh fruit, vegetables, meat, fish, cheese as well as clothes, bags, and antiques. They are usually held on the same day each week.

Buses carry people from place to place along city streets. Double-decker buses have two floors. Bendy buses are like two regular buses joined together, one behind the other. Some buses take you on a guided tour of the city and usually have an open-top roof.

Construction Site

A construction site is a noisy place! Engines rumble, saws whirr, and drills whine. Trucks bring building materials like bricks and girders. A concrete mixer churns concrete into the pump. Then the pump pours it into the pit to make the foundation. Workers shout instructions as the crane hoists materials to make the top floors of the new building.

Site office

Scaffolding

Concrete mixer

Flooring

Pump

Spreading concrete

A dump truck carries rubble away from the site. It is a huge vehicle with giant wheels. To empty its load, the back tilts up and the rear gate opens.

Every building site must have one of these! This is a portable toilet. The builders are on site for only a few months, so a permanent one is not needed.

When the walls of a building are completed the plasterer gets to work. He adds water to the plaster powder to make a dough-like mixture. Then he spreads it on the wall. It dries to a smooth, hard finish.

Crane

Pump

Bulldozer

Digger

Girders

Clearing rubble

Dump Truck

A digger can scoop up rubble in its bucket and drop it into the back of a dump truck.

Carpenters make door and window frames. They use electrical tools to saw wood quickly and easily.

Glaziers fit glass in the new building. In some modern buildings, whole walls are made of glass. It has to be cut and placed very carefully.

Many modern buildings are built not with brick walls but with steel girders. These are lifted into position using cranes.

Farm

It is near the end of the summer. There is lots of work to be done on the farm. The chickens and pigs need to be fed and the barn must be stocked up with fresh hay bales. The children are having a horseback riding lesson.

Sheep

Orchard

Chickens

Stables

Plow

Horses

Pigsty

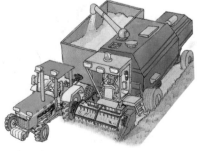

Using its wide cutting wheel, a combine harvester cuts the stalks of wheat as it trundles through a field. The grain is stripped off and emptied into a trailer.

A tractor is a powerful vehicle that can pull a plow or other farm machinery. Its huge rear tires make it easier for the tractor to move in muddy fields.

Apple-picking takes place in the fall when the apples are ripe. Some farms are open to the public and let visitors pick their own fruit and vegetables.

Milk truck

Cows

Cowshed

Barn

Hay bales

Tractor

Trailer

Grain

Rabbits

Tractor

Combine harvester

A milking machine is used to milk the cows. Only one farm worker is needed to operate the machine. It is much quicker than milking by hand.

Plowing and harrowing prepares the soil for the new crop. A plow turns over the top layer of soil. This brings nutrients to the surface. A harrow tills the soil ready for planting.

The horses on a farm must be cleaned and groomed regularly. The stable hands brush them and give them water. The horse's tail swats away any pesky insects!

Clock

Information board

Station

Exit

Ticket office

Metro

Café

Information kiosk

Passengers visit the information kiosk to find out the times of trains, how they can reach a certain place, whether they must book seats, and how much the fare will cost.

The information board shows when the next trains will be leaving. It also tells passengers if their train has been delayed or canceled.

A guide meets the tourists at the station platform. Holding up a flag for them to follow, she leads them to the bus that will take them to their hotel. There are often bus stations near train stations to take passengers on the next part of their journey.

It is rush hour at the train station. Some people hurrry to catch their train, while others have time to sit and wait in the café until their train arrives.

Train

Pantograph

Platform

Buffers

Electric motor

Tourists

At airports and large train stations you might see baggage carts like this one being pulled along by an electric vehicle. Passengers' luggage can be loaded onto the train more quickly using these.

The metro station is located under the main station. Metro lines crisscross the city under the ground. Because they avoid the traffic in the streets, metro trains are often the quickest way to get around town.

Trains are powered by electric cables that run above the tracks. A device on the roof of the locomotive called a pantograph collects the electricity, which then powers the motor inside.

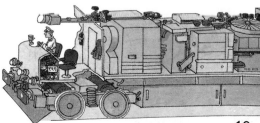

Crane

Container ship

Container

Fishing trawler

Tugboat

Warehouse

Fishing vessel

Refrigerated truck

Though it is small, a tugboat is specially designed to tow heavy ships, such as oil tankers. It has an extremely powerful engine that drives a large propeller under water. Tugboats are built with a strong steel hull and rubber bumpers to push ships.

A crane is used to hoist containers from trucks parked on the wharf onto the ship. Some cranes move along on rails, so the same crane can load different parts of the ship.

Gulls can be seen and heard around fishing ports. They fly above the boats and wait for their chance to steal some of the day's catch.

Crane

Hoist

Port

A port is where ships load and unload their cargo. Big containers and crates have to be loaded onto trucks using cranes. The goods inside these containers are stored in warehouses on the wharf. Fishing boats also dock here to unload their catch.

Train

Stow-away

Mooring

Forklift truck

Wharf

Forklift trucks can carry very heavy loads in tight spaces. The forks can lift crates off the ground up to where they can easily be rolled on to a van.

Customs officers sometimes check goods arriving at a port. They are looking for illegal cargo, such as drugs. Sometimes they find stowaways!

After goods arrive in port they are carried overland by train or by truck. The goods are then unloaded in a warehouse.

Index

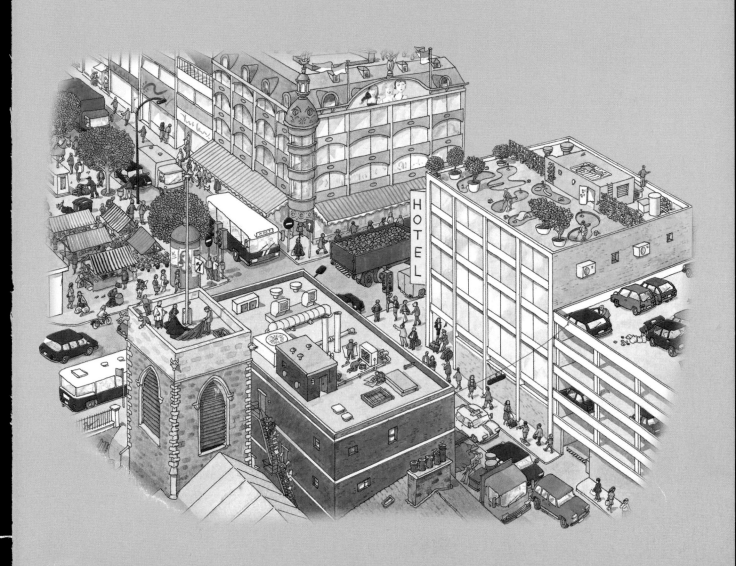

Did you find him?

pages 6-7

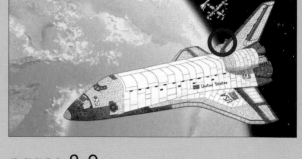

pages 8-9

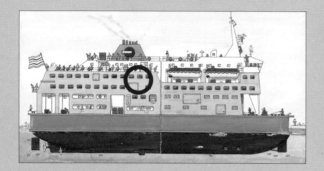

pages 10-11

pages 12-13

pages 14-15

pages 16-17

pages 18-19

pages 20-21

For more great fiction and nonfiction, go to www.windmillbooks.com

24